The Corn Snake

Understanding and Caring for Corn Snakes

BY

DR. GORDON ROBERTS BVSC MRCVS

Table of Contents

Introduction
What Is A Corn Snake?
Is The Corn Snake A Good Choice Of Pet For You?
Getting A Corn Snake
Housing A Corn Snake
Feeding A Corn Snake
Corn Snake Breeding
Understanding Corn Snake Health
The Behaviours Of Corn Snakes
Conclusion

Hello! My name is Gordon Roberts and I'm the author of this book. I hope you enjoy all of the specialist advice it contains. I'm a huge advocate of preventative care for animals, and I'd love to see more pet owners taking the time to research their pet's health care needs.

Being proactive and educating yourself about your pet's health now, rather than later on, could save you and your pet a lot of trouble in the long run.

If you'd like to read more of my professional pet care advice simply go to my website at http://drgordonroberts.com/freereportsdownload/.

As a thank you for purchasing this book, you'll find dozens of bonus pet care reports there to download and keep, absolutely free of charge!

Best wishes,
Gordon
Founder, Wellpets

INTRODUCTION

The most popular choices of pet in the UK are, of course, cats and dogs with over 17 million in the country. But some people are interested in the wilder, somewhat intriguing animals that come under the "exotic" category. This guide is all about corn snakes. In the UK, it's estimated there are around 400,000 pet snakes and this accounts for approximately 0.3% of British households. These numbers are likely to increase with the growing emergence of interest in pets like snakes.

The understanding and care of a corn snake cannot be compared to the understanding and care of cats or dogs. Corn snakes are exotic pets with exotic origins and their needs and traits are wildly different. This is why anyone who wants to get a pet corn snake will need to research and understand exactly what is required to look after such an unusual creature.

In this guide you will begin by getting a feel of what a corn snake is, what they look like and where they come from. From then we will ask the question: "Is the corn snake a good choice of pet for you?" – and we ask this because, although they appear appealing and different compared to a more common pet, you will need to look after them far differently to the way you would look after the more typical pets.

You do not want to make the mistake of buying a corn snake on impulse, to later find out you cannot provide the care it needs.

Advice is given in this guide regarding how to source a reputable supplier of corn snakes and how to select one properly. Once you know about this and, before you take your snake home, you need to know all about the kind of accommodation your snake requires to live happily and how to correctly feed them.

You get the added bonus of breeding information in this guide, as it's becoming a popular hobby for people to breed corn snakes. Obviously, this needs to be done correctly and you will need to know exactly what to expect with breeding.

Being a caring corn snake owner means you need to know about their health. You need to know when your snake is in poor health or good health, and you need to know how to spot any health problems. You will also be shown the most common health issues corn snakes in particular may suffer from. Corn snakes, just like any other pet, are at their happiest when healthy.

Corn snakes behave vastly different to other animals and such an unusual animal will behave in ways you may not be familiar with or understand. Our behaviour chapter will guide you through the common behaviours of corn snakes, so you get to grips with why they behave the way they do without being confused.

WHAT IS A CORN SNAKE

Corn snakes and their origins

Corn snakes are a constricting and non-venomous species of snake found in the eastern and south-eastern parts of the United States of America. They can be found in various states, such as New Jersey, Florida, South Carolina, Louisiana, Kentucky, Tennessee, Georgia, North Carolina, Texas and Virginia. They can also be found in smaller concentrations in other states, too.

They belong to a family of snakes called "colubrids" or "colubridae" - a group of snakes that are non-venomous and make up nearly 80% of the Earth's snake species.

Natural habitat

They are found in various habitats in the wild – woodland, hills, farmland, roadsides, fields of tall grass and even unused buildings. They are able to climb trees and other elevated areas, but they also venture on the ground and search burrows, logs and other places for prey. At a young age they keep to ground level, but after four months they are more likely to inhabit higher areas, even cliffs.

Their name – "corn snake" - comes from the storage method performed by farmers. They would harvest the corn and keep it in wooden frames or log structures. Rodents would often find their way into these places to feast on the corn. This meant it was a perfect spot for corn snakes to frequent to prey on mice and rats.

Appearance and anatomy

A corn snake is considered medium in size, with new-borns being approximately 12cm in length, and adults ranging from between 60cm to well over 180cm. Their body is not considered as wide and large as pythons, for example. Corn snakes are more slender in build.

Their colours are very striking and bright with the most common colours being orange, brown and red. They can also have fragments of black and white. The colourings and patterns can vary quite a bit according to the location the corn snake came from and its age. Colourings as not as vivid in hatchlings, but patterns become brighter as they increase to adulthood.
If you look at a corn snake you will notice the lack of an appearance of an ear. Though there is no ear seen externally, corn snakes can hear using a bone connected to their jaw. This makes the hearing of vibrations on the ground easy.

You may also notice they do not possess eyelids. Their eyes are, instead, protected by a transparent scale that sheds just like their skin, and their eyesight is adapted to noticing movement in the wild effectively.

It's a canny mix of their hearing, vision and impeccable sense of smell that makes the corn snake experts in finding and hunting prey, as well as dodging threats.

A prominent feature of any snake is their menacing tongue. It's vital for the corn snake to detect scents by gathering the scent's molecules. Their Jacobson's organ then processes the molecules to determine what is being smelt.

Corn snakes have impressive mouths. The jaws have an elastic quality to them, making animals easier to break down and swallow. The work of their jaw, teeth and throat forces the prey down into the digestive system. Though unpleasant to witness, a corn snake has the physical ability to digest prey wider than their own bodies. You can find out more about feeding corn snakes in a later chapter.

Their body is structured by ribbed backbones and they are highly durable while being flexible at the same time. Having a body this shape also means internal organs are placed differently.

It may seem strange how a creature can move without limbs. Corn snakes, as limbless animals, use their elongated bodies in a certain way to move. They are actually more versatile and clever with motion than you think any creature without arms or legs would be! The different ways of movement are shown below.

Types of snake movements:

S-s-s-serpentine: Much like an S-shape movement and involves the corn snake contracting the muscles while moving the body from one side to another. The purpose of this is to create a succession of curves. This movement is used to travel in water and land. On land the snake can advance further by using natural elements from the earth as pushing points, e.g. rocks, bumps, undergrowth, etc.

Concertina: Used in smaller areas where space is limited or to climb. The snake's body curves to such an extent that it can grip onto a surface while the snake pulls or pushes with other parts of the body towards the desired direction.

Caterpillar: A slow movement also known as rectilinear motion. The body contracts into curves, but this time they are smaller and the snake's body curves upwards and downwards instead of side to side – just like we see with caterpillars.

Sidewinding: A snake in an environment with very few points on the surface to use for movement may adopt the sidewinding movement. Much like the serpentine motion, they contract the muscles while leaning their body into an S-shape, but this time only two areas of the body make contact with the earth.

Corn snake trivia

- Corn snakes in the wild can live between 6 and 8 years.
- There are multiple colour morphs of corn snakes, such as "Miami Phase" (grey, red, orange and black), "Candycane" (red and orange markings on white), "Bloodred" (solid orange or red), amongst others.
- There are also various pattern morphs, such as stripes, inverted spotting and other unusual and eye-catching patterns.
- Out of all the snakes held in captivity, the corn snake is one of the most popular.
- Some snakes can live up to 23 years in captivity.
- Corn snakes are often used to control rodent infestations and keep rodent populations down where they pose a threat to crops and health.

Is the corn snake a good choice of pet for you?

A question that genuinely needs to be answered before you go any further. The care and appeal of snakes is immensely different to what you might expect from a more popular choice of pet.
What to expect

Firstly, your corn snake will require suitable specialist housing with suitable heating, lighting and in-house objects. It needs to be a good size and you need to be able to maintain this housing properly and regularly.

You will also need to feed your corn snake a diet slightly different to the canned stuff you'd buy a dog or cat, so you need access to a supplier that caters for snake diets. Their diet will also involve feeding times that are not as regular, so you must keep note of how often and when exactly you feed the snake.

Corn snakes behave and have needs and natural habits that differ from other animals, so you'll need to grasp a decent understanding of hygiene, housing maintenance, the right foods and storage, handling the snake properly and so forth.

Ask yourself these questions:
- Do you have the space to keep a corn snake?
- Can you afford the cost of foods, running their housing, pet insurance and other care costs?
- Are you a reptile kind of person? Will you take joy in caring for their needs?
- Do you know where to obtain the right foods and how you would store it?
- Do you know enough about creating and maintaining a suitable habitat?
- Are you confident in handling a corn snake properly?

- Does everyone else in your household want a corn snake and will they know how to care for them the right way?
- Do you have access to a vet that specialises in reptiles?
- Do you have the time in your day to day life to care for a corn snake?
- Can you be dedicated to their care for their entire lifespan?
- Can you make suitable arrangements if you are temporarily unavailable to look after your corn snake?

You cannot take the decision of owning a pet lightly. We're talking about a real, living thing and a lasting commitment from you. A pet corn snake, like any pet, will have many upsides and downsides and it will be helpful to know about these in order to form a decision. Here they are below.

Advantages of having a pet corn snake

Normally, if you want a pet corn snake you will experience individual benefits to having them according to your likes and individual views. Corn snakes come in a large variety of colours and patterns, which means when choosing one you are highly unlikely to know anybody else who has one looking the same as yours. Having a pet snake – not to mention a unique looking one – will mean you have a not-so-conventional pet and lots of snake owners are proud of this.

Compared to various other snakes, a corn snake is more slender in build and a decent size that isn't tiny, but isn't too large either. This means they are generally quite easy to handle once you get used to them (and they get used to you!) In fact, many snake enthusiasts say the corn snake is one of the best kinds of snake to handle, with very little chance of being bitten.

Lots of people view snakes as aggressive, vicious, scary, defensive killers that will bite, constrict around anything living and attack human beings. This largely warped view probably comes from the representation of snakes in film, television and other forms of media. It also comes from the fact that the average person can only recall the most venomous and dangerous types of snake because their features and behaviour are easier to remember and are represented more in films – remember Indiana Jones being lowered into a pit of snakes in Raiders of the Lost Ark and being faced by a very angry cobra?

In reality, a corn snake isn't as terrifying as you might think. In fact, their temperament is considered to be very calm and they deal with being handled and interacted with without hostility. Being a non-venomous snake with the ability to become tame are two traits that also make human contact easy and safe. This makes them a suitable choice of snake to have as a pet.

Though you will always need to make time for any pet, regardless of which animal it is, the corn snake won't require the constant interaction a dog or cat will need to be content. Corn snakes are wired differently and their wellbeing is not dependent on being overly social. This means they are less time-consuming in this regard.

Their general care may be not as costly compared to other pets. The investment into their housing and maintenance may appear expensive, but everything else is less so. For example, they do not need to be fed several times each day. Feeding is normally once a week and only involves placing a small dead mouse or rat into their habitat.

So, let's have a quick overview of some of the advantages of having a pet corn snake:
- Plenty of choice on colourings and patterns
- A unique pet
- A suitable size to keep as a pet

- Can be easy to handle
- Good, calm and tame temperament with very little chance of biting
- Won't require the levels of social interaction compared to other pets
- Day-to-day care is simpler and usually inexpensive

Disadvantages of having a pet corn snake

Corn snakes may have a natural schedule different to yours. Being what is called "crepuscular", they are at their most active at dusk and dawn times. Through the day time the snake is probably going to want to sneak away for a sleep. This will mean you're more likely to have the opportunity to interact during dusk or dawn, or alternatively you will need to turn the lights down and block out any daylight to encourage your snake to liven up.

Purchasing the suitable housing for your corn snake may cost you a bit initially, and then you must know how to effectively maintain it so your snake has a habitat it feels happy and comfortable in. Their movement capabilities and body mean they are expert at escaping. This means the habitat you provide must be carefully examined for any small gaps your snake could escape through.

As mentioned in the advantages section, corn snakes don't need to be overly social. People normally get pets because they enjoy their company, so keep in mind that corn snakes are not the most social creatures. You may not get the reactions and behaviour you would expect from a cat or dog when showing affection or interaction.

If you're squeamish, corn snakes are not the right choice for you. A slithery, scaly animal that gets its elasticated jaws around a dead rodent isn't what everybody wants to witness. You will need to enjoy them as animals and be confident in handling them, as well as dropping dead rodents into their habitat with no problems.

Speaking of rodents, you will need to know where to get them and how to store them. Storing dead rodents may be tricky to do hygienically.

There is a chapter on feeding later in this guide. The cost differs – you are saving money in the sense that you only need to feed the snake once a week, but the mice will cost a little more to buy.

When a corn snake is tame, handling is easy. But the snake needs to be tamed first and this takes patience. You will also need to introduce handling gradually, which also takes time. Taming an adult corn snake will be more time consuming compared to a younger one, and purchasing an adult will cost more, too.

If you have your heart set on a specific morph or appearance, you may find looking for it a lot trickier than approaching selection with an open mind. So, be prepared to choose something you like because of its availability instead of its specificity.

Here's an overview of the disadvantages of having a pet corn snake:
- Corn snakes have a different body clock to you
- Habitats are costly and need to be run properly
- Corn snakes can easily escape from their habitats if it's not sealed appropriately
- They are not overly social and don't interact like other pets do
- Squeamish people will not enjoy having a pet corn snake
- Their food might be costly and storage can be difficult
- It will take time to tame a new corn snake
- Finding a specific colouring or pattern will be tricky

So, there you are. If you're still not sure, take your time. It's a big decision to make and the last thing you want is to rush into something that you will regret. The general feel is that if you're 100% certain you want a corn snake, you should get one.

If there is still uncertainty after a while, it's best to say no for the time being and see how it goes. Such an unusual pet won't be the perfect choice for absolutely everyone! Just be sure to do the research and know for sure you are ready and prepared for a corn snake and have an understanding of what to expect.

GETTING A CORN SNAKE

It's time to look at the actual event of getting a corn snake. Firstly, you need to know where to get one and what guidance to follow. We'll also look at what preparation is needed before you bring your new pet home and what you will need to do when your snake is settling in. For more detail on the specifics of corn snake care, you can find chapters later in this book informing you of suitable housing, feeding, breeding, health and behaviour, which will be hugely beneficial to read up on before you get your corn snake.

Finding your future corn snake

The same rule will apply here as it does with those finding a breeder of puppies or kittens – choose someone reputable, preferably with good recommendations from others. You may want to do some thorough research on the internet and ask questions on snake related forums about specific breeders in your local area. Your vet may be able to recommend a breeder or somewhere that will have that kind of useful information.

You won't find any luck capturing a wild corn snake in the UK. They originate from America, and it's strongly recommended not to capture one from the wild anyway. You must, instead, source one that has been bred in captivity. A corn snake bred in captivity will have a temperament used to being around people and their health won't be affected by the stress of being detained.

Choosing your corn snake

When you meet the breeder to choose your corn snake, remember to ask for the snake's history, which should include health, shedding and feeding record – this ensures there are no problems with the snake's overall wellbeing and shows the breeder is genuine and reliable with nothing to hide.

You need to know whether you want a hatchling or an adult. Hatchlings might be easier when it comes to becoming accustomed to certain routines, such as being fed frozen rodents. Adults, however, will be ready for breeding and hatchlings will not. If you want to see your snake grow up and teach it the ways of the world, go for it. Deciding on a hatchling or an adult corn snake is entirely up to you.

Observe the snake and make sure to handle the snake before you buy it. This is a good way of finding out about the snake's health and what their temperament is like.

The snake should:
- Be alert
- Able to eat their food without any issues (and you should ask to witness this)
- Have no signs of bad health (check the health chapter for more details)
- Be relatively docile
- Have bright eyes
- Be able to flick its tongue often
- Have a clean, smooth, rigid skin
- Have no signs of poor appetite
- Have no signs of leftover shedding on their body

Ask the breeder lots of questions and if for whatever reason you are in any doubt, do not press on with the purchase. You've got to be sure they are healthy snakes. You also need to be sure the breeder is willing to keep in good contact with you, even after the purchase, for advice or to answer any questions you have. That is when you know they are reputable.

Colourings and patterns are entirely your choice. Corn snakes come in various appearances, most of which are striking and beautiful, so you will definitely see one that takes your fancy.

Transporting your new corn snake home

You can transport your corn snake home as long as the journey is relatively short. You can keep your snake in a firmly secured bag made of cloth. A smaller sized corn snake may be transported in a secure plastic container with a lid with adequate ventilation and paper. If the journey is more than an hour, keep the snake in the bag inside a secure box containing paper shreds and, again, ventilation. Temperatures should be between 21-24°C. Hotter temperatures could be fatal.

Becoming acquainted

Advice on housing can be found in the housing chapter later in this guide, so be sure to read up on getting the right kind of habitat ready to introduce your corn snake to.

Having such a placid temperament means corn snakes are the perfect snake for first timers. Handling will come easily and their non-venomous nature means they are less likely to react to you with aggression. In fact, when scared, a corn snake is more likely to want to hide than take a swipe at your hand. Just never assume they definitely 100% won't strike at you. Calmness is key.

They may be a little nervous or stressed at first, as they are coming into a new environment and being handled by new people, so be aware of this and be gentle. If they rattle their tail, this is usually a normal reaction for a snake that hasn't settled in yet. It will ease off when they get used to their surroundings and feel more secure. Try and keep them as comfortable as possible.

Handling should never be too much too soon. Keep it at a steady pace and begin handling in brief periods, trying to avoid stress or rough handling. Once your snake behaves more at ease, you can increase the handling duration bit by bit.

Basics of handling

Once your corn snake is adjusted to being handled by you and other family members, you can begin to put handling into a routine. It's generally advised to handle your snake for about 10 to 15 minutes per session for around 3 or 4 times each week. Some snakes may require more, some may require less. It depends more on the individual snake, so observe their preference.

Corn snakes, as they would be in the wild, will need to be active, so spending time outside their little habitat will benefit them hugely. When you do take them outside, handle them carefully. You must make any children aware that the snake isn't a toy and will need to be held gently and properly. Hold them in a supportive manner so you are not at risk of letting them fall from your hands. A poorly handled corn snake will be stressed out and very unhappy.

Their mood should normally be docile when you are handling them, making them one of the easiest snakes to handle. If, for whatever reason, they are startled in any way, you must take them back to their habitat. A startled corn snake is more likely to feel nervous or defensive and strike out, though this shouldn't be a problem if handled correctly. Always supervise children when they handle the snake. Any children 5 years old or under should not handle the snake at all, or you may even need to reconsider having a snake if you have children this age.
Importance of hygiene

Before you handle your corn snake, you and anyone else handling them will need to wash their hands with an antibacterial wash. You will need to do this immediately after handling, too. A multi-snake household requires hand washing to decrease the chances of spreading infections from one snake to another. Not everyone knows, but many snakes can carry salmonella. Corn snakes commonly carry salmonella without showing any signs of it. This can quite easily infect humans and make them sick. Hand washing is therefore extremely important before and after handling or handling any snake-related objects. Ensure your children wash their hands thoroughly.

Keep your snake away from areas where you prepare food and avoid using kitchen facilities to clean your snake and their cages and objects. Even where your snake slithers, be sure to clean the area afterwards. If you keep to a strict and thorough hygiene routine the likelihood of getting salmonella dramatically decreases.

Quarantine and a multi-snake household

If you already have pet snakes, wondering whether you should keep them together is a head-scratching dilemma. The general view is that it depends: Corn snakes are solitary creatures and will have no problems being in a habitat by themselves. Some people can keep more than one corn snake together without there being any issues, but others end up in stressful situations and need to be kept apart.

Many snake owners feel keeping two captive female corn snakes together will be okay, but two males may be a problem with increased chances of aggression – in this case, it might be worth keeping them separate. You should also avoid keeping a male and female together unless you intend to use them for breeding purposes.

If you plump for keeping your snakes together, it's recommended to keep them in quarantine for a few months, preferably in different rooms. Keep hygiene standards high by washing your hands before going from one snake to another to avoid passing on anything infectious. Quarantine is recommended not only to ease off unwanted behaviour, but also to ensure your newbie snake is healthy and not contagious. Your vet may want to check their health and advise you on the exact rules and durations of the quarantine.

HOUSING A CORN SNAKE

Your new corn snake needs to feel at home with the right habitat to live in. Let's have a look at what you need to set up and maintain for your newbie pet.

Good sizing

Lots of people think snakes need massive enclosures to move around in, but for corn snakes it's quite simple. They like to be a little bit active outside their housing, but when they are inside it they prefer a lower level of activity. They are at their most content in a moderately sized vivarium with the floor sizing up to about 1 square foot per foot of the snake, with a general height of the vivarium matching a third of your corn snake's length.

If you have a hatchling, do not keep them in the size of an adult vivarium and this may cause them to become stressed out by the large size. Instead, give them a smaller one. If they show signs of poor appetite or stress, the habitat may be too large.
Secure vivarium and lid

As mentioned previously, corn snakes are escape experts! Their vivarium needs a firm lid that does not crank open easily. It should have some kind of mechanism on it to keep it clasped into place to prevent any escapes. Don't assume the lid is secure enough because it can shut down properly – you'd be surprised how strong a corn snake is!

Correct hygiene

Corn snakes defecate a few days after their weekly meal, meaning it's not as regular as other popular pets. General cleaning is therefore quite straight forward and will not be needed on a daily basis. Cleaning consists of clearing away any defecation, disinfecting any objects and the inner walls of the vivarium, but use a safe and diluted disinfectant or cleaning product designed specifically for reptile housing hygiene.

Substrates

Substrates are hygienic, absorbent shredding or shavings used in the corn snake's vivarium to ensure a comfortable environment they can safely move upon and burrow under. The most recommended types are aspen shavings, unprinted newspaper layers (not with ink as this is harmful!), paper towels, coco or orchid bark or artificial grass. Some of these may be off limits to your snake depending on humidity levels, so check with the breeder or vet before choosing one. Some substrates are advised not to be used at all due to their toxicity, e.g. cedar and redwood shavings.

Fresh water

Corn snakes need fresh supplies of water every day. Use a heavy bowl in a moderate size and ensure it is not light enough to be moved and tipped over by your snake. It's used not only to drink, but also as a bathing tool for when your snake is shedding. Do not leave the water bowl contaminated with the snake's elimination. It will require a disinfection and water replacement straight away.

Heating

In the wild, your corn snake would get all the heat it needs from its natural surroundings. In your house, however, it's a little different! A corn snake would normally practice what is called "thermo-regulation" – where they shift to different environments with different temperatures according to how hot or cold they are. For a cold blooded animal, getting the right amount of heat from the environment is crucial.

The temperature needed in your vivarium should be within 21-30°C. And this is normally supplied by a heat mat including a thermostat or, alternatively, you can use a specialist bulb with a dimming controller. These will need to be designed specifically for corn snakes, so find a reputable pet store to get the right equipment.

If you're using a heat mat, it only needs to be over half or one third of the vivarium flooring. This is because if your corn snake feels too warm, it can thermo-regulate as it would in the wild and go to another part of the vivarium to cool down. Having one covering the whole floor means they cannot achieve that and an overheated snake could prove fatal. This heat mat needs to be connected to a thermostat to control the temperature and prevent any overheating occurring.

You may instead prefer to use a bulb fixed to the vivarium roof. Like the heat mat, it's also connected to a stat, but this one controls the dimming level to keep a healthy temperature. A naked bulb is not a healthy option and could burn your snake, so you must use it with a bulb guard.

This option is often less preferred, however, as corn snakes will be extremely unhappy in a constantly lit environment, but the lighting is necessary for keeping the right temperature – this is why the heat mat is a better choice. If you use a bulb, then discuss how to use it with your vet to keep a good temperature while keeping your snake happy at the same time.

In-house objects

Corn snakes need an imitation of their wild habitat. They use natural objects to hide in, to climb with and as aids to move around effectively. Keeping some in-house objects is an absolute must.

Corn snakes are surprisingly submissive and will definitely require some kind of formation in which to hide in. It will be a structure to help them relieve stress and it can be created by yourself or bought from a versatile pet store. Homemade items that make good hide-outs include small card boxes, used kitchen or loo rolls, clean plant pots turned upside down and various other items. Use your imagination!

Just make sure it's a safe material, that it has a decent archway made on the side so the snake can enter and exit easily, and that it's a good size – enough space for your snake to curl into, but enclosed enough for your snake to feel secure and protected. It's worth having two of these hide-outs – one in the cool area and one in the warm area.

The floor needs not only substrates, but a few items to create a mixed texture. Corn snakes in the wild use points in the earth to use against their bodies in order to create effective locomotion – little rocks, small branches, bumps, etc.

Corn snakes need items to use for effective climbing, too. Branches, rocks, fake plants and similar items are good for movement, climbing aids and help the snake shed its skin. Take care if you bring in rocks and branches from the wild – they need to be disinfected, rinsed and dried to kill off any nasty parasites and other bacteria. Be aware that specific plants are dangerous to corn snakes, so ask your vet before using any.

Corn snakes need stimulation

Again, remember the imitation of the wild theme and think of the kind of environment your corn snake would be in if not captive. They would be exploring new areas all the time, so try and rearrange and change the scenery in their vivarium occasionally. Maybe even add and replace objects from time to time.

Snakes are naturally inclined to explore and be curious about their habitat. They need their surroundings to change so they can achieve this and be stimulated. An empty or unaltered layout for them would make life very boring and everybody wants a happy snake.

Humidity

You need to be careful with humidity as you would with other factors like temperature. Humidity at a low level can cause your corn snake to have issues with shedding, but a temperature too high can cause health problems, too, such as the damp causing skin conditions or respiratory infections.

Ventilation can affect the humidity levels of the vivarium – less ventilation creates more humidity and better ventilation causes less. Humidity will be higher if you supply your corn snake with a large water bowl. Humidity can be increased or kept at a particular level by putting the water bowl on the heat mat or warmest area. It can be decreased by putting the bowl in the coolest area.

Lighting

If the vivarium has a spot bulb, then this can be used for lighting and appearance purposes. Lighting would be purely for viewing reasons, as corn snakes don't need UV light. Too much light, in fact, can be problematic for your snake. The use of a well-protected 2% UV tube can be used for viewing purposes only. Make sure any lighting bulbs emit low levels and are surrounded by a secure guard to prevent your snake curling around it and getting burnt.

Natural light should be allowed as corn snakes need a life involving natural elements of the wild. Natural light will help your snake with their body clock. If you use bulbs instead, they should be switched on and off according to the natural light and darkness of day – off at night and on when morning comes – to imitate natural light routine. Always keep check of the vivarium's temperature if you have bulbs inside. Overuse of bulbs may cause an unwanted increase in temperature if you have bulbs inside. Overuse of bulbs may cause an unwanted increase in temperature, which will be unhealthy for your corn snake.

Ventilation

Most vivariums designed for corn snakes will feature plastic or mesh grids to give the crucial circulation your snake needs to survive and be healthy. The grids should feature at various heights inside the vivarium, so air can enter and exit successfully for effective regulation.
Features of a vivarium can vary. Some kinds can include grids as part of the lid and this is generally considered as a good way to improve airflow. You can also get fans for the vivarium that are attached to thermostats or timers – these can be quite handy because they can turn on when air becomes too warm.
Other general maintenance

It's advised to keep two logs for your corn snake. We mean the ones you write! Keep note of vivarium maintenance: when you clean out and alter their vivarium and make a routine of checking the running of the vivarium – the heat sources (mat or bulb) should be checked, the temperature and thermostats should be monitored, the humidity and ventilation should be checked and so on. This is just to ensure that everything is running smoothly and their habitat is safe and suitable at all times. It also ensures any problems or faults can be identified quickly. The second log includes health matters - when you feed your snake and how they take it appetite-wise. It should also include when your snake sheds their skin, their weight and their length which should be checked every now and then. This is, again, basically a good way to refer to something if any issues arise.

Housing overview

Don't feel too daunted by all the elements listed regarding your snake's housing. Once you get the hang of it, it will be easier to understand and maintain. The important thing is that if you keep the habitat at a suitable level, your snake is going to be healthier and happier, not to mention more stimulated. This will help them live a longer life and remain your slithery friend for many years to come.

Here's an overview of what is required housing a corn snake:
- A vivarium the appropriate size according to your snake's length
- A secure habitat with no large openings or easy-to-open lids
- Regular cleaning and disinfecting of the insides and contents
- Regular changing of scenery and replacing safe substrates often
- Fresh water every day in a sturdy bowl for drinking and bathing
- Safe and regulated heating equipment in specific areas
- Hiding, climbing and exploratory objects
- Safe regulation of humidity
- An approach to lighting that doesn't negatively affect your snake
- Proper ventilation
- Keeping logs for maintenance and health

If you have a problem with the housing or you're not sure about anything, you can find sources of information to troubleshoot your issue online, via online communities of corn snake owners, reptile organisations, or your vet will happily help.

FEEDING A CORN SNAKE

Feeding a corn snake isn't as cutesy as you'd probably want it to be, but for some it's a fascinating and unusual thing to witness. With feeding, like it is with housing, you go along with a mimicking of natural routines. In this case, you must feed your corn snake dead prey.

A question you should ask yourself before getting a corn snake is whether you are confident and not squeamish when it comes to handling, storing and feeding dead rodents. For some this is simply out of the question, so remember what kind of unconventional needs have to be catered for when purchasing a corn snake.

In this chapter we will answer a few common questions regarding feeding corn snakes.

What do I feed my corn snake?

The safest and easiest meal to give your corn snake is dead mice. You may be able to find other similarly sized dead rodents in certain pet stores, but mice are the easiest to find. These other rodent choices include small rats, hamsters and gerbils. Dead chicks are also possible to feed your corn snake with, but rodents are considered to provide the nutrients your snake needs.

The required mouse size is according to the corn snake's mouth size – give them a mouse the similar width of one and a half times the snake's head size.

These rodents will be dead. It's strongly advised never to feed your snake live animals. It's not humane to throw a live mouse to a snake to eat, but it's also not fair on the snake because there is always a risk of the rodent scratching, biting and defending itself during the kill. Never ever feed your corn snake wild rodents. These pose a high risk of carrying parasites, disease, infections and even risk killing your snake from the rodenticides. Only source your rodents from reputable pet stores.

How do I store their food?

The rodents should be kept in a freezer, but obviously store them securely away from any human foods. You can buy them already frozen and it's recommended to thaw them thoroughly before feeding them to your snake. You can defrost them by keeping them in a secure plastic bag for a couple of hours, but ensure this is away from any human food preparation areas and out of reach of children or other pets.

How do I feed them?

One dead adult mouse should be given per feed. Larger corn snakes may require two mice per feed, or could prefer larger rodents such as baby rats, small hamsters or gerbils. The breeder who supplied your snake may be able to recommend which type of meal your specific snake prefers. It's best to feed the rodent using clean tweezers of some kind. Invest in something to grip the mouse in order to safely place it for your snake to eat. This is recommended because the scent of the mouse may be present on your hand if you use them. Though it's rare, the corn snake may mistake the rodent scent on your hand as their meal and strike out. Be aware your corn snake is at risk of digesting the substrate in their vivarium if you feed them in there, so take care about giving the rodent and try to feed away from the substrate or even outside the habitat. Large amounts of substrate being accidentally digested may cause health problems.

After feeding, it's best to leave your snake for a while without handling or you might find your snake bringing their recent meal back up again! Some snake experts suggest periods of 2 days after feeding to leave your snake before handling can commence again.

How often do I feed my corn snake?

Each feed should occur about once a week, but often 10 to 14 days can be okay. Once the feed is complete, make a note in your corn snake diary so you know when the next feed is due and how well the snake is taking their food. For hatchlings, this routine may be different. Refer to the hatchling and adult snake question below for more details.

Are hatchlings fed differently to adult corn snakes?

Yes, because corn snakes need to be fed according to their size. Hatchlings should begin with pink mice – these mice that are new-born, smaller is size, softer and easier to eat, are still hairless and compliment the size of a hatchling to be able to digest properly. Feed one of these to your hatchling every 5 to 6 days.

When the hatchlings grow, you can begin to change from new-born pink mice to young mice with fur and, later, bigger and older mice. Remember when this transition occurs, you must start feeding them a little less often and start to feed as if an adult corn snake.

How do I know if my snake is being fed too much or too little?

Overfeeding, just like with humans, is shown by the snake gaining weight. A corn snake fed too much too often may become obese and this could end up being fatal.

As a corn snake owner it's recommended to check the length and weight of your snake occasionally and to make a note of this. Keeping a note of this information will flag up any changes so you know if underfeeding or overfeeding is occurring. If you're still really unsure, speak to your vet or ask the breeder who you purchased your snake from. They may know more about the background of your snake.

Also keep a log of the feeding schedule and feeding habits, which includes how the snake takes the food. You can then make matches with this information with the weight and length information. If your snake is ill from what you suspect to be diet related, see your vet straight away.

What if my corn snake won't eat when I feed them?

Let's start by troubleshooting this for hatchlings – hatchlings are more inclined to not take their food well because the initial prey for new corn snakes in the wild will not necessarily be rodents. They are also naturally inclined to detect prey by their scent and/or by seeing them.

A reluctant hatchling can be helped to eat again using a number of techniques:
- Avoid over-handling your snake as this will cause it stress and poor appetite
- Remove the scent from a baby mouse by washing it and then place it inside the vivarium for your hatchling to discover it
- Rub the mouse softly on a pet lizard or put the lizard's shed skin around the mouse to change the scent into something less volatile, then feed it to the hatchling
- Encourage the wild hunter side of your hatchling by rapidly moving and dangling the mouse in front of the snake's hideout using a long holder implement – not your fingers!
- Sit down, hold the hatchling softly but firm enough and very gently touch their nose with the dead mouse to encourage the snake to strike – then sit there until its digested before placing the snake back inside their vivarium and leave them for at least 48 hours

- Hold the snake and softly try to open the hatchling's mouth with a dead mouse by adding a very mild pressure to the mouth – when the snake opens it and covers some of the mouse's body, jolt the mouse very slightly to allow the snake's teeth to grasp onto it, then leave them in their vivarium for a few days

For adult corn snakes you can use a few of these techniques above – the most effective being something called "tease feeding".

Tease feeding, as mentioned above, involves you moving the dead rodent as if it were alive. Again, we are imitating the wild elements of a corn snake's life here. But you need to be careful, as you are encouraging your snake to break out their hunting instincts and strike. So, use a long holding implement such as tongs or tweezers with long handles. You can buy feeding tongs especially for this procedure.

Make sure you move the mice as if you were rapidly scurrying a toy in front of a cat to pounce on. Make the movement stop and start in an unpredictable way, combined with slow movements and swift ones. And, of course, make sure your hands are nowhere in the vivarium! Some ways are simpler than others. Many corn snake owners find that leaving their snake for a few more days, or even a week, is enough to get their appetite back again for feeding. If you notice their appetite does not return after this, you know there is something wrong.

There are various reasons behind your corn snake being reluctant about feeding – they could be shedding, being handled too much in general or before or after meals, they may be in poor health, they may be fussy about the temperature of their food, their temperature might be too high or too low, the food may have lost its scent, the food may be incorrect or the wrong size for the snake to digest, or the snake may be too stressed or anxious and go off their food as a result.

You can gather and find out how your snake is doing and often why their appetite has changed by keeping a feeding, health, vivarium maintenance and shedding diary, recording all the information about how often they eat, their state of appetite, their behaviour, the temperature and humidity levels and when they have shed their skin.

Corn snakes can go off their food if they have shedding and dehydration problems, so always provide fresh water every day for drinking and bathing. They also go off the food if they are experiencing a digestive problem or poor health, and at this point you should take the snake to the vet.

Make sure you are feeding the snake as required for hatchlings and adults – this includes how often you feed, the kind of feed and the size of feed. Sometimes corn snakes refuse their food because it's the wrong time, the incorrect food or the rodent is too large for them to properly digest.

Sometimes it comes down to food preparation. People have the habit of doing things conveniently quickly, but defrosting a mouse with hot water just because it's quicker to do may take away the scent needed to draw in the snake for feeding.

Be reminded that imposing anything too forceful in order to get your snake to feed may cause even more stress for your pet and make the problem worse, so be gentle always.

What happens if my snake regurgitates their food?

This could happen for a few different reasons. Firstly, your corn snake may have been given a rodent a bit too large for them to fully digest. Think about finding some smaller mice and adhere to the approximate sizes mentioned earlier in this feeding chapter. Remember rodents are sold for snake feed in various sizes and the size must correspond to the snake's size. So, if you're giving a hatchling an adult mouse instead of what is called a "pinkie" or hairless baby mouse, then there's your problem.

Another reason could be the temperature. Sometimes the temperature of the vivarium can affect your snake's wellbeing enough to decrease appetite and the ability to digest properly. This is why recording all this information is so vital, as well as keeping check of the temperature to ensure it's the correct level.

Regurgitation is often linked with digestive woes, parasite problems or other health issues. You need to have contact with a pet that specialises in exotic pets so you can bring them in for a consultation and check-up. A common cause of regurgitation is over-handling. As a loving owner, it's natural to want to be in contact with our pet corn snakes on a regular basis.

Unfortunately, many owners tend to handle their snake too much, making them increasingly agitated before a meal and ruining their appetite. They also tend to not wait long enough after their snake has eaten. It's like you eating a big dinner and being tossed around immediately afterwards – not nice! So try and leave your snake alone for at least a few days after their feed.

Stress can cause regurgitation, so think about what the trigger could be. Is it handling? An unfit habitat? Other snakes sharing the vivarium? Being handled incorrectly? Having a vivarium that's too large or too empty? Are they well? Is the vivarium suitably controlled to the right temperature? Do you or children pester the snake a lot? Do you invade their habitat a lot? Do you make loud noises or tap the vivarium walls?

Though corn snakes only need feeding about once a week, they are ravenous when it's feeding time. A snake with a healthy appetite will just go for it when presented with a rodent at feeding time. But sometimes it's just too tempting to give them more than they need and many corn snakes are being overfed. Overfeeding can cause regurgitation.

Do corn snakes need water?

Yes, they do. They will require a large water bowl in their vivarium. This should be a hefty weight, as the movement and slithering of a corn snake would otherwise easily tip the bowl over and lead to zero water access. Change this water at least once a day.

Corn snakes need water to drink, but they also need it to bathe in, which is particularly vital to assist them during shedding periods. No water will cause dehydration, poor shedding and poor health as a result.

Is it safe to leave my corn snake alone if I go on holiday?

If you go away for no longer than two weeks, you are quite safe to leave your corn snake. Any time longer than this will require someone to look after them.

Corn snakes don't necessarily thrive on being social like other pets do and they are content enough to be left alone for a week or two. Ensure to feed them just before you leave and as soon as you get back, but the snake will definitely need access to lots of water. You can buy water controllers that refill water bowls on a timer when you're not there.

Your snake will benefit from having someone visit occasionally to check on them – this is just as a precaution if any problems arise with themselves or their habitat. It's good to be safe, rather than sorry.

CORN SNAKE BREEDING

It's a popular, easy and common hobby for many corn snake owners to keep more than one snake and to breed from them. Thousands of corn snakes are hatched every year and those numbers are rocketing as you read this.

The great thing about breeding corn snakes is that many people comment on how simple it is, how unique an experience it is and how exciting and fascinating it is to witness. So, if this is something that interests you, keep reading!

Why people breed corn snakes

Many people breed corn snakes simply as a hobby and these kind of snakes in particular are very easily bred compared to other animals and reptiles. For some, this hobby gets quite intense – many people take great interest in the beauty of corn snake colourings and patterns and there is heightening popularity in their genetics and the many morphs of the corn snake.

Others take pleasure in breeding corn snakes because of the overall process and that selling healthy hatchlings and adult snakes can remunerate them for the cost of breeding them. Liking the money-making side is fine as long as you look after the snakes well and sell healthy pets in an ethical and honest manner.

Finding out which are male and female

Male corn snakes differ from females. Males are generally larger and features will be different, such as the tail shape. There are a few methods to be sure of your corn snake's gender below:

Probing: Probing is a technique used for sexing a corn snake regardless of their age, but it does require precision and a gentle approach or serious damage, even infertility, can occur.

Probing involves using a specialist probe to discover what is called a "hemipenis" – this is part of the male's overall reproductive system called the "hemipenes". This is found near something called a "cloaca" near the tail area and the organ, instead of protruding outwards, stays inside when it's not being used. The lubricated probe is used while someone holds the snake's body upside down. The probe should be gently entered underneath the cloacal scale and pointed towards the tail tip in order to discover the opening, Due to the complicated and risky nature of this procedure, it might be worth asking an exotic pet vet to do it for you.

Males are identified by the probe successfully going down the hemipenis and the depth of this is normally slightly more than the width of the snake's tail base. Females will not have a hemipenes and the probe won't go down as far.

Popping: Popping is the safest and easiest way to sex a corn snake when compared to probing. It must be done gently to avoid any damage being done. This procedure is only recommended for hatchlings.

You need to hold the snake belly up with the tailed positioning upwards where the anal opening is located. Put your thumb near the tip of the tail, but not right near the end, and past the anal area. Roll your thumb – don't slide – forward towards the anal vent. The thumb movement should evert the red coloured hemipenes and it will go back inside once you remove your thumb.

A female will not present any hemipenes, but instead will show two red coloured spots – one on one side of the vent and one of the other side. Comparing sizes: You can compare the length and shape to determine the sex of a corn snake. Males will exhibit longer tails compared to females. The male tail will also be broader due to the presence of their hemipenes near the vent area. Females have shorter tails, with narrower width at the vent area.

Where to start

Obviously you need one female snake and one male snake. Corn snakes need to be a minimum of 75cm long before they are suitable for breeding. In order to get things off to a good start, it's better to hibernate your snakes beforehand.

Your snakes will need to be fed well, with special attention given to the female who will need to prepare herself biologically for around 5 to 7 weeks once hibernation is completed. This is a time where her body organises the ovaries in order to create eggs. For this to occur healthily, a good diet full of nutrients is required.

How to hibernate your snakes

You can either change the temperature of the habitat to mimic a winter cooling or prompt a full hibernation period before breeding commences, and it's generally advised to do so.

A winter cooling is achieved by changing the temperatures in the vivarium to decrease your snake's day cycle. Day time temperatures are recommended at 24 - 28°C, and night temperatures are recommended at 19 - 21°C. This can be done for around three months and feeding can be reduced during this time. When fed, the snakes in their winter kind of state will only want smaller meals, but fresh water changed daily will always be needed.

Full hibernation can be achieved by avoiding a feed about two weeks before hibernation begins and then placing the snake into a well-ventilated box containing a safe substrate. The box needs to be kept somewhere with a consistent temperature of 10 - 13°C. This needs to commence for around 90 days. Be careful about the temperature. If the temperature drops too low or too high beyond the bracket suggested it could be very dangerous. Keep the water there and ensure it is fresh.

You can check on them every two weeks to see if they're okay.
After full hibernation, your snakes will need plenty of fresh water and a feed around two days after the end of the process. These feeds must be plentiful in order to gain a decent and healthy weight needed for breeding.

The act of breeding

When hibernation is completed you can bring the two snakes together again in the vivarium, ensuring the temperatures are 24 – 29° C. The act of breeding is likely to begin once the female corn snake sheds her skin. Her sex pheromone will entice the male to begin breeding activity which is shown below:

Chasing: After the male picks up the female pheromone the "wooing" will begin. During this time it's common to see the two snakes engage in rubbing, pushing or nudging, movements and touchings with the two tails, body movements, tongue flickering and the male will also want to put at least some of his body over the female. The vents at some point will align and contractions can occur to help the mating along.

Alignment: This involves the tails gradually aligning beside each other. This ensures their reproduction organs are in the right place to mate with. The tails will start to wriggle and spasm while the male's hemipenes enters the female in order inseminate.

Intromission: Once insemination is completed, the hemipenes will leave the female and the two snakes may, for a short period, stay entwined. The act of breeding may occur several times over a few days, but the act done just once can often be enough to be successful.

Ovulation

A truly intriguing fact about corn snake breeding is that the female is capable of storing the male's sperm for some time, so mating is able to occur before ovulation is even happening. The female can use the stored sperm when her body is ready to ovulate and eggs are ready to be fertilised. This is what makes breeding easier and more convenient for corn snakes compared to various other species.

If you wish to wait until the female snake is ovulating, you can spot this period of time by noticing a swelling of the second half of her body. Scales may protrude a little.

After breeding and laying eggs

The male and female are allowed to remain together for a few days after mating and then be separated, or you can keep them apart straight away. The male will need several days' separation from any other females after breeding has occurred. If you notice any problems with the hemipenes retracting, keep the male in a habitat with little content for a short while. The vivarium they mate in should temporarily have its contents removed during and after the breeding to prevent injuries. A male showing signs of injury around the hemipenes will need veterinary attention.

The presence of eggs depends on the biological status of the female during breeding – if she was ovulating during breeding then it will take a little less time compared to whether she wasn't. This could range between 20 to 45 days and you will notice she has eggs due to her size becoming fatter.

She may shed during this time, but when this is complete she will want to find a warm, safe location to lay the eggs where humidity levels are at their most suitable. In order to provide this kind of location, you may want to provide a medium plastic box with a hole on the top wide enough for the mother to come and go as she pleases.

The box needs a substrate inside that won't make the insides too damp, but will retain humidity. Within this box, she will make her own alterations in order to form an environment safe and comfortable enough for egg laying.

The number of eggs to expect can vary, from as little as a handful, to many dozens. You may find after a few months more could be laid. The gathering of all the eggs together in one bulk is called a "clutch". They start off involving soft eggs, but these soon become firmer with pale colouring to them.

Incubation

A complete clutch needs incubation almost immediately – within a day. These eggs are extremely fragile, however, and eggs moved around and upside down will be fatal to the contents. So, when moving eggs into an incubator occurs, never rotate them and be extremely gentle and steady. To avoid confusion of which is top and which is bottom, spot the top with a pen. If you're wondering if anything is going on inside these eggs or not, you will be able to tell by the growth. The eggs will get bigger. You can use a bright light to check for contents when you shine it through, but don't be too alarmed if you cannot spot anything obvious, as it may not be developed enough to show anything up.

Your incubator needs warmth, so try and obtain one that comes with a bulb, heat mat or other kind of heating implement that connects to a thermostat. You may also need a thermometer as a precaution and a humidity regulator, such as a hygrometer. The temperature and humidity needs to be detected in the same location of the eggs.

The incubator should be small, well ventilated and contain a safe, hygienic and absorbent substrate, which is where you will carefully place the eggs. This incubator container should have some details marked on it regarding the parents, dates and other useful bits of information. Incubation occurs typically from 45 to 90 or so days, but duration is dependent on the temperature. The eggs will be incubated between 21 - 32°C.

The egg hatching moments

The final days of incubation may alter the positioning of the eggs and within a day or two the eggs will hatch. The hatchlings will break their way out of the eggs using their noses, but this may be a bit of hard work for the hatchling and you must allow them a day or so to break out completely. Trying to help them out should be avoided as you are risking a serious injury to the snake.

If the eggs don't hatch or die this could be due to an inappropriate temperature in the incubator. A humidity below or above 70 to 90% could also cause death or no hatching. And finally, poor ventilation can also cause bad results. The eggs need oxygen, so make the incubator a ventilated one.
Congratulations!

If all went well and you've got your new hatchlings, you can now begin their general care which is highlighted throughout this book. Remember that their care depends on their size, so hatchlings will require smaller habitats and feeds.

UNDERSTANDING CORN SNAKE

Making sure your corn snake is healthy is a vital element to being a snake owner. You need to recognise a healthy snake, recognise when they are in bad health and know a bit about the common health problems corn snakes can suffer from. Recognition can help you understand your snake's health, keep them healthy, prevent poor health and aid you in spotting when things aren't right. Healthy snakes are happy snakes!

Signs of good health in corn snakes

Corn snakes are usually reliably healthy when given the right diet, care and habitat. You will notice a snake in good health by witnessing the following:
- Strong, muscular body that is a good round shape that thins out at the tail
- Bright, clear eyes
- Clean, firm, smooth scales
- Curled up, relatively anti-social temperament is nothing to worry about
- A typically calm temperament
- Good appetite
- Clear mouth and nose

Signs of bad health or habitat problems

- Skin that remains on the snake during shedding in rough pieces
- Sneezing or wheezing
- Discharge from nose or mouth
- Skin folds
- Obesity or ribs showing
- Puffy or swollen areas of the body when not breeding
- An accumulation of substance around the mouth
- Wounds on the body
- Poorly structured spine
- Sign of parasites
- Prolonged poor appetite or consistent regurgitation

Shedding

This is a perfectly natural process that involves your snake shedding its skin. Shedding occurs more frequently in young and growing corn snakes. During shedding your snake's eyes may change in colouring and cloudiness may appear, but this is perfectly normal. Their scales will dull a little for several days and their appetite might change during this time. The snake will probably locate to moist areas of the vivarium, such as the water bowl, as wetness aids the shedding process.

The shedding will normally occur as a whole, but sometimes snakes shed their skin in pieces or unshed skin may remain. This is likely to occur because the vivarium's humidity levels are too low. Be observant and gently bathe and rub skin excess that hasn't come off.

Blister disease

Blister disease is present when your corn snake's skin has white blister-like or bubbly appearances to it. It's down to their habitat being poorly maintained. A dirty vivarium that isn't cleaned regularly as well as dirty water that isn't changed every day can cause this skin condition. It could also be caused by poor humidity levels – the substrate may become too moist and the humidity levels may be too low. Your snake may recover after a few sheds if you change the substrate may become too moist and the humidity levels may be too low. Your snake may recover after a few sheds if you change the substrate more often with better, safer, absorbent substrate, clean the vivarium thoroughly on a regular basis, change their water regularly and decrease the humidity levels.

Severe blister disease is very dangerous and may require more intensive care from yourself by attending to each blister by draining it and cleaning the skin every day for a week or two. An exotic animal vet will advise you on what solution to bathe the skin with and how to do it effectively, if you're unsure.

Parasites

Yes, corn snakes can get them too! Ticks, mites and internal parasites can be present in corn snakes, but this is happening less and less the more corn snakes are bred in captivity. The parasites come from the outside world, but don't think your snake is safe just because it lives indoors. If you feed them rodents you found from the wild or bring in any natural objects to put in the vivarium you may be bringing your snake something infested with parasites. Do avoid this, only buy your feed from reputable stores and disinfect, rinse and dry out anything before placing it in the vivarium.

Internal parasites will need the attention of your vet, but ticks can be removed at home. You can use some specialist tick tweezers to grasp onto the tick head and rotating so the tick unscrews from the snake and is released. Do this hygienically and dispose of the ticks safely. Ticks can also be killed off using prescribed sprays.

Mites can be caught easily from snake to snake and vivarium to vivarium, but they also spread disease! Their habitat needs to be treated and cleaned and repeated after nine days to eliminate any hatched mite eggs. There are mite sprays to use on your snake and the vivarium which, again, needs to be repeated after nine days.

Some types of parasites are a lot more dangerous, so you need to act pretty quickly if you notice anything different about your snake.

Respiratory problems

Corn snakes only have one lung that functions as you think a lung should. This is why respiratory problems are more common and must be treated very quickly. Snakes that exhibit signs of wheezing and similar problems need to be taken to the vet for treatment as soon as you notice them. Snakes with respiratory problems will need to be quarantined away from other snakes in a habitat that's in another room. This is because some conditions are contagious. The conditions of a habitat may have something to do with respiratory issues, so check the temperature and humidity are at the healthy levels and take any veterinary advice seriously.

Stress

Corn snakes can experience stress, believe it or not. This is less common in captive corn snakes, but still able to occur. Some snakes become stressed and hide for long periods of time for reasons such as their vivarium being too large and too empty – corn snakes like to feel secure. Refer to the housing chapter of this guide. Stress can also occur through poor handling, whether it be clumsiness or from being too aggressive while holding your snake. They also become agitated if handled too often, especially immediately prior or after meals, which can also cause food rejection and regurgitation or vomiting. Keep their vivarium clean, the right size and with a good variety of items and places to hide. The habitat husbandry should be maintained correctly and you should respect the fact they need alone time. Keep them separate from other snakes if stress occurs and keep the vivarium somewhere where there is not an abundance of noise and activity.

Mouth rot

Snakes with a caseous substance around or within their mouth may have mouth rot. It can be present on the gums, lips, throat, noses and in other areas in close proximity. It can also include ulcers and inflammation. It's a bacterial or fungal infection and will need to be treated effectively by a vet, particularly if it has progressed to a severe level.

Abscesses and burns

Burns are prevented by having protected guards on bulbs and other heating implements as well as keeping them at the required temperature. Snakes can curl around an unprotected bulb and burn themselves without realising it. Burns will need some attention by a vet. Abscesses are normally caused by an injury that isn't treated and leads to a bacterial infection. You can notice an abscess by its appearance, which is a lump under your snake's skin. To verify the presence of an abscess, and not something else such as eggs or a tumour, your vet will need to examine it and then give the suitable treatment.

Obesity

Corn snakes are susceptible to obesity and this is purely down to overfeeding. It's a common thing for people to give into the delight of seeing their pet enjoy their meal– so much so they are inclined to feed them more because they think it's cruel not to. In fact, feeding your snake more than you should is only going to cause problems.

Corn snakes don't need the energy and diet that many other animals need, so overfeeding just gives the snake more of what it really doesn't need. It leads to obesity and obesity alone can cause lots of other health conditions. Get your corn snake to lose weight over a gradual period of time by steadily changing how often you feed your snake, the size and the quantity of the feed. Do not starve them as this will make their health deteriorate. If you need advice on diet and nutrition, speak to your vet.

Constipation

Corn snakes in captivity are more likely to get constipation. It can be caused by a number of things – wrong vivarium temperature, dehydration, being injured, being unwell, parasites or being dried out causing complications. Having ample water and access to it for bathing purposes will help constipation in your snake. You can allow your snake to bathe in warm water for a brief period of time every day for a couple of days to help. If no defecation occurs still, see your vet.

Eye problems

Corn snakes can suffer from eye problems due to abnormal shedding or infections. Such a vital organ will need veterinary attention if you notice any injury to the eye, problems with the skin or any abnormalities.

Cancer

Tumours can occur on the snake's body and, as with other animals, tumours can be malignant or benign. To assess whether the tumour is cancerous you will need to go to your vets for a formal diagnosis. Any lumps found on your snake should be treated with suspicion, just as a precaution. Tumours can occur in the snake's body tissue or any of its organs.

Egg binding

Egg binding is typically a secondary problem and is seen in female corn snakes. It involves swelling in the snake's body in the shape of eggs or a general swelling. Change the temperature and humidity and if there is a lack of a nesting location, create one. This should help encourage healthy laying of eggs. If this doesn't work, contact your vet.

Bacterial and fungal infections

Various conditions can occur due to bacterial and fungal infections. These are commonly the result of unsuitable temperatures, bad diet and nutrition, wounds, unwanted humidity and overly moist environments, so their vivarium will need adjustment and a visit to the vet is recommended so suitable treatment can be given.

Digestive problems

Problems or abnormal defecation, poor appetite, diarrhoea, weight loss, problems digesting food fully and sickness or regurgitation are all common signs your snake has digestive problems. They can be viral or bacterial when it comes to infection, or involve something related to their habitat or the food in question.

Handling your snake less and ensuring it isn't too stressed or agitated will aid appetite. But a poor appetite that continues to persist will need to be checked out by a vet. Prolonged digestive problems can cause some serious damage, so don't shrug it off and hope it will go away.

Salmonella

As mentioned earlier in this guide, the bacteria belonging to salmonella are present within the gastrointestinal location of your corn snake. This is normal and will not cause any symptoms or poor health. In rarer cases, salmonella strains can build up more than usual and cause a digestive disorder, but this is unlikely if the habitat operates at the correct temperature, the snake isn't stressed and the food is safe and not infected.

Salmonella is a risk to humans, however, and can make us very sick. This is why thorough hand washing with antibacterial wash is required before and after handling corn snakes, as well as before and after touching any snake-related objects.

Young children should not be allowed to handle the snake as their immune systems are not as strong as adults and their sense of hygiene isn't as strict and putting hands in their mouth is common. Older children must be supervised when the snake is handled and always insist on hand hygiene. Also avoid handling your snake in the kitchen and don't clean your snake or wash its vivarium and contents in the kitchen where food is prepared.

The health conditions mentioned above are just a few common examples of problems a corn snake can encounter with their health. There are too many other issues to mention, so it's important to seek your vet's guidance when you notice anything abnormal with your snake. Various problems such as obesity can cause secondary conditions, so spotting anything unusual must be acted upon.

Many health issues can be avoided by:

- Maintaining a clean habitat
- Keeping healthy temperature and humidity levels and checking them regularly
- Providing clean water every day
- Feeding when required with the correct type and size of feed
- Not bringing in any wild feed or objects that pose a parasite or disease risk
- Being hygienic when handling more than one pet
- Being a generally caring, observant snake owner
- Attending to any wounds by keeping them clean
- Find a vet that you know specialises in exotic pets

The Behaviours of Corn Snakes

Such a unique pet choice is bound to exhibit some natural behaviour you may not be accustomed to, so it's great to understand your snake better by having an awareness of their behaviour and why they do the things they do.

Temperament

A corn snake will behave according to its overall temperament. Luckily, corn snakes are docile animals, particularly compared to other snakes, so their general even-temperedness makes them a good pet choice. Other snakes such as pythons or boas are more likely to become a little too big for people to cope with.

Their temperament means the likelihood of you being bitten is low. Many corn snake owners remark on their pet as having a very likable personality, with the tendency to slither away in their hideouts instead of confront you if feeling threatened.

Tail rattling

Why would a corn snake rattle their tail? We often associate tail rattling with angry venomous snakes who are feeling very defensive, but the perhaps more pleasant and friendly corn snake can still rattle their tail. They do this as a warning that they feel threatened, but this is more likely to happen compared to being viciously bitten, and is geared more towards something they consider to be a predator. You can ease the tail rattling by being calm, gentle and allowing your snake to grow more familiar to your company and handling. The more used to you they are, the most secure they feel, and the rattling stops.

Little noises

It may not necessarily sound like hissing, but some corn snake owners report hearing hissing, spitting, whistling or unusual breathing sounds from their pets. The cause of this depends on whether they are feeling defensive or stressed out. You are more likely to hear noises when you first get a corn snake and they are stressed out due to not adapting to their new surroundings yet. These snakes are best left alone for a while. Whistling, wheezing or any other noises that sound like unusual breathing could be a sign of a respiratory problem, and this will need to be addressed by a vet quickly. Remember corn snakes have only one fully functioning lung, so don't waste any time.

Basking

Corn snakes enjoy heat when it suits them. In the wild their heat source would be the sun, though you will need to provide other sources of heat for a corn snake living in a vivarium. Basking is a behaviour where the corn snake savours the direct sunlight in order to gain warmth. In the wild this would be a very common behaviour, so it might be a good idea to allow them some natural sunlight so they can keep doing this.

Defensive corn snakes

A corn snake, particularly an adult one, should normally be more easy-going about being handling and being near humans. Ones that do not experience regular handling such as juveniles may be more inclined to behave differently by being wary and defensive.

Their nervousness may make them want to strike out at just about anything that comes near them, including your hand, and this is just a natural defensive behaviour at this stage. The behaviour should ease off after time when they learn you are not harmful or a threat.

Biting humans

As mentioned several times in this guide, corn snakes rarely bite. If they do, it's normally because they feel threatened by you. The bite isn't particularly bad and you should experience minimal pain. Some snakes may bite because of your own hesitance. If you are feeding your snake, especially for the first time, you may feel a little apprehensive about their reaction.

Some snakes may bite because of your own hesitance. If you are feeding your snake, especially for the first time, you may feel a little apprehensive about their reaction. Hesitance may result in your feeding hand moving erratically in front of the snake. You want to move it close enough to feed the rodent, but you are scared. This kind of movement, however, may instinctively make your snake view your hand as prey.

The erratic movement is similar to seeing a live mouse move about in the wild. This movement could incite the hunter instinct, or even make them fearful or angry and want to strike.

Biting can also occur in snakes that are yet to learn to trust you as their owner, or it could occur because during a feed the prey's scent is on your hands and they strike out of confusion.

Biting other snakes

Biting from one snake to another can occur out of aggression. Corn snakes are not big fans of being in the company of other corn snakes. Two rival males are the most likely to be aggressive to one another, and this aggression can consist of biting and pushing at each other. Another form of biting, ironically, is used between a male and female during mating. The male may want to bite her head or neck as a form of courtship.

Tongue flickering

All snakes flick their tongues. They will do this very often and it's perfectly normal. Their tongues flicker because it's how your snake tastes the air in the environment to know what is around them. This is where their Jacobson's organ takes in particles that the flickering tongue has accumulated. This allows them to figure out what and where any potential prey would be or to discover their surroundings.

Hibernation

Hibernation is not essential for corn snakes and usually occurs if the snake cannot perform thermoregulation properly due to the temperature being too low. Hibernation, otherwise known as "brumation", can involve the corn snake being inactive somewhere hidden and avoiding regular feeds.

Check on your corn snake if you notice this, as brumation can be mistaken for being ill, vice versa. If you wish to know how to bring on hibernation for breeding purposes, refer to the breeding chapter of this guide.

Constriction

Constriction is when a corn snake wraps itself around its prey to subdue and suffocate it. It tightens around and adds pressure to the prey. This act is performed in order to weaken or kill the animal in order to eat it. You won't normally see a lot of constriction as captive corn snakes are usually given dead prey at meal times.

Movements and climbing

Corn snakes move cleverly. A limbless creature such as the corn snake is remarkably good at using its body, its sense of locomotion and its scales to move in different ways and climb effectively. More detail on this can be found in the "What is a Corn Snake?" chapter near the beginning of this guide.

Burrowing

Corn snakes take pleasure in burrowing due to their inquisitive nature and tendency to want to hide and feel secure. Substrates in their vivarium can be used to burrow in, as well as little housing hideouts.
Behaviour changes and wellbeing

Sudden or strange behavioural changes may be connected to the corn snake's wellbeing. Snakes may change their habits when not well or experiencing the effects of a poorly run vivarium (e.g. incorrect temperature, too much lighting, unsuitable humidity, etc.) Behaviour can also change if they feel nervous or stressed from something. Snakes can change their mood and feel not particularly happy. Try and identify the cause and contact your vet if you suspect poor health.

Day and night behaviour

Corn snakes like to be inactive during the day and rest or hide. You are most likely to see more activity from them as evening and night time comes around. Their nature is nocturnal as in the wild discovering their surroundings during the night would be a suitable time for hunting. Each snake is different, however, and you may find variations to this behaviour.

Corn snakes are at their most active during the warmer months and this is when they are at their most nocturnal. So, if you want to play, interact or handle your pet corn snake, remember that fun times are appreciated a lot more in the evening.

CONCLUSION

By now, hopefully, you will have a bit more knowledge and understanding of your pet corn snake, or at least what to expect and how to prepare for getting one. Though, the act of caring for your corn snake will bring more knowledge through experience.

An unconventional pet will bring you plenty of intrigue and joy, but their needs will be unconventional, too. Keeping good contact with a vet that specialises in the treatment of exotic pets is advantageous, especially as not every single veterinary professional will have the expertise and experience of reptiles.

A running theme in this guide has been the imitation of the wild – mimicking what a corn snake would have needed in a wild, non-captive environment. Corn snakes cannot be domesticated to the point of being like a lap dog, so providing care that closely matches the elements of the wild is vital for their wellbeing.

Your relationship with your corn snake will improve the more you know how to care for them. This relationship is important right from the word go. This is because your snake's state of mind depends on how well it trusts you and whether it feels secure around you.

Part of this relationship involves your understanding of what your snake needs and what it doesn't need – so, for example, you may know your snake needs lots of branches and hide out dens in its habitat… but you should know also that, for example, your snake doesn't need to be handled excessively.

The majority of corn snake owners absolutely adore having one. Though it's a common misconception for people to view corn snakes as frightening or too wild, for people like yourself corn snakes are fascinating, friendly, easy-going and distinctive creatures to make part of your family.

In fact, lots of corn snake owners start with one and end up with what they call an addiction and end up with many more! You can understand why, what with the simplicity of breeding them and the alluring appeal of having such a strikingly beautiful and exotic pet.

There are plenty of sources to acquire further information about corn snakes. You can obtain details from the snake's breeder, from an exotic animal vet, peers with snakes, or from the internet where you will find a surprisingly large online community of corn snake owners and enthusiasts who share and advise each other from their own experience.

Remember your snake is an individual and they can live for some 20 years if well looked after, so you've got yourself a friend for a long time. With good care your corn snake will repay you in its own special way by being a brilliant and interesting pet for many years to come. Embrace and enjoy it!

Want to know more about looking after your pet?

The writer of this book, Dr. Gordon Roberts, is a veterinarian and owns a total of eight animal hospitals around the UK. He believes that the key to a healthy, happy pet is preventative care, which is only possible when pet owners take the initiative to educate themselves about their animals. As a result, Gordon has written dozens of useful reports on pet care in order to share his years of experience with discerning pet owners. As a thank you for purchasing this book, you can browse and download his specialist reports completely free of charge! You'll learn all sorts of useful information about how to spot possible health conditions early on, and how to make preventative care for your pet a priority, helping you save time and money on visits to the vet later on. To view and download these bonus reports, simply visit Gordon's website at: http://drgordonroberts.com/freereportsdownload/.

Best wishes,
Gordon

Made in the USA
San Bernardino, CA
29 April 2019